13 8

by
Mark Maier

Published by DSM Story Forge

Copyright © 2022 DSM Story Forge

All rights reserved. No part of this publication may be reproduced, distributed, or transmitted in any form or by any means, including photocopying, recording, or other electronic or mechanical methods, without the prior written permission of the publisher, except in the case of brief quotations embodied in critical reviews and certain other noncommercial uses permitted by copyright law. For permission requests, write to the publisher, addressed "Attention: Permissions Coordinator," at the address below.

ISBN: 979-8-9861562-2-4 (Paperback)
ISBN: 979-8-9861562-7-9 (eBook)

Any references to historical events, real people, or real places are used fictitiously. Names, characters, and places are products of the author's imagination.

Book design by Joe Deptowicz (joe@winmorecolumbus.com)

Published by DSM Story Forge, LLC in the United States of America.

First printing edition 2022.

DSM Story Forge
1733 Boulder Court
Powell, OH 43065

www.dsmstoryforge.com

Dedicated to David and Laurel
    Thank you for living your story
So that I may share mine

CONTENTS

3 A.M.
Last Night
Uproot
The Night Before I Die
Holding
Haunted
Westbound
Winter Solstice
Soul Jumper
Zoo
Crazy
Emerging
Dreaming With Open Eyes
Internal Peril
Mental Well Being
Fade
Nirvana
Appointed Time
Reestablish
Good Enough
In A Room By The
Window So Close
Doomsday
Beauty
Defined
'Til Death

Sanity

When I'm Gone

Troubled Sleep

Impressive

Come And Gone

Reliability

Almost

Should

Like Thoughts Crowding My Mind

Inevitable

Life

Wayne City

Mystical Fish

Three Oh Five

Bitter

Collected

Room Without A View

Paper Doll Princess

Rest

Cleansing

No Doubt

S.O.S.

13 8

Jeremy

Timely Touch

Before The Dawn

3 A.M.

What is so fascinating
About the hour at hand?
The time comes around
At the same strike
Of the clock each day.

But I am here – awake – alone.
And eating a simple supper
On this brisk November
Friday morning – or maybe
This is Thursday night
(Liable on who is asked) –
But technically this is Friday,
Since the time is after
midnight.

The moment is early, careful.
Depending on a lot of criteria.
But here I am and maybe,
Just maybe, someone else
Is also awake in this moment.

And the time is spared
In sharing in pairs, or peace,
Or multiples there within,
Or thereof.

Oh – forget the technicalities.

Welcome to this moment –
No matter how asleep
Or awake you remain.

Last Night

This is the eve
Of Adam's downfall
When the license
For his green thumb
Is rescinded.

Uproot

I found
I cannot move,
For too many roots
Are holding me down
Within this societal orb.

Cut me out!
Set me free!
To fly –
To endure –
Without ties –
Without straps –
Without obstructions.

Come out from behind
These four walls.
Come out from behind
These confining fears.

Every moment
I am secured down
These roots
Grow double,
Locking me in
Even deeper.

Reveal to me
The axe,
So these foundations
Don't hold me
In place
Anymore –
Cut me free
Before this
Becomes my
comfort.

Bring freedom
To this soul
For movement –
For advancement.

The Night Before I Die

I wanted to live, to stay alive, breathing in everything in that moment and remembering the past while dreaming of the future, the next few hours or the next few moments, all while standing alone or surrounded by those who claim they love me, and listen to the stories carried by the winds, and to add a few stories of my own on the breeze, over the creeks of the building still settling, until the last gust of the night fades away, and the final breath is carried right along with it, to the distant land or into oblivion.

Holding

God, why can't I
Feel you holding me?

God, why am I
So numb?

Why not
Take me from
This place
Of unknowing,
Of uncaring?

Why am I
Too paralyzed
To squirm?

Why should I
Be holding out?

What have I got
To lose with You?

I don't know
What the answer is,
So that is why
I just question.

Haunted

I don't know what
I need to do
To make things
Better.

Everything my hands
Touch becomes cursed
And fall apart.

There's a raging
Maniac inside
Who wants out
Of this prison?
But there's
No understanding
Of how to
Be released
Peacefully.

The smell of rain
Just before dawn
Brings back
Haunting memories –

The past that
Should have been
But never was.
There is something
Sane about
All the madness.

Maybe, just maybe,
This is sensory
Overload –
But is that what's eating
The spirit slowly?

I want to stand
On the edge
Of a cliff,
Ready to jump
To Hades below –
Stretch my arms
Like an eagle
Gliding –
Maybe the trip
Through hell
Will get me
To heaven
Somehow,
But that's not
How that works –

Not this time,
Not ever.

While the dog
Next door
Barks into
The emptiness
Of night.

Westbound

Driving across states
With an influx of vowels -
Ohio
Indiana
Illinois
Iowa -
Before settling in
For a constant…

Good night.

Winter Solstice

I'm found living
Within my own
Utopia of solitude.

Underneath the twinkling
Stars decorating the sky –
An escape to loneliness.

Maybe this is a getaway
To avoid global pandemics
Of religious factions

Bashing each other
For their personal uses
Of religious traditions.

All-encompassing tribal
Warfare nullifying the time
Of peace on earth

And goodwill towards
Other human beings
For being unhuman.

I keep my doors locked
To avoid the cold infiltrating
The warmth I'm hoarding.

I'm closed off to a bitter world
For the simple pleasure
Of enjoying the offerings

During the worn-out
Wonderland
Of a silent night.

Soul Jumper

I want to leave.
Want? No.
I need to leave.
Just get in the vehicle
And drive away.
Unstoppable –
To lose myself
On the open road,
On the labyrinths
Of highways, byways,
Freeways, roadways
Zigzagging
Across the country.
Stopping only
For stories
At rest stops
And gift shops,
Fast food joints
And scenic points.
This soul unbridled –
No walls that limit,
No doors for closure,
No fence-lines to stop.
I'm not running
From anyone
or anything –

Those debonair misfits

Can think whatever

They want.

But the words

Spewing from their mouths

Usurps their true

Validity.

They might say I can't

Live without them,

That I need them

For my survival

And then they might say

They don't need me,

That they've made it

Without me,

As though I am one

Of their peons

Working, sweating,

Undulating

While seeking

Minimal payback.

Their minds

Would explode

In a colorful array

Of flatulence.

I'm not seeking

Payback –

I put that behind me.

The time has come

To move on

And not

Hold back —

Forward motion —

"Don't look back"

Is the new freedom mantra –

Based on an old refrain.

And I should

Enjoy this time

Of open-hearted,

Free spirited

Clairvoyance.

This is how

I would change

History –

Not by a national

Standard,

But by the standard

Of one man

Or woman

At a time.

To have and to hold

And to build

'Til death

Does he depart

From the worldly

Unprogressive possession.

The road we must travel

With no confinements,

However it may bestow

Upon this tour

A few practical

Detour signs –

Life is under

Construction

After a series

Of deconstructing

Moments.

We are all

Headed

One way,

A means to an end –

Glory, glory

Hallelujah –

Jump in the car

And keep on

Keeping on –

Driving or

Riding

With the windows

Up … or down –

The open road

Is free for all,

And a free for all

Because

Taxes paid
Tolls made
Slight grade –
An inclination
To slow it down
Or speed it up –
Giving time
To take
Another breath
Of life
On the exposed
Pathways
Carrying the prayers
Of a simple man
Having the life
Of a God with a plan
As I fight
Through praying.
For the continued
Liberation
Of humanity
Believing isn't
Always seeing
At first.

Zoo

I have a window seat
At the café.
I watch the walkers,
The stalkers,
The shoppers,
The business folks,
The parents pushing strollers,
The children pushing parents,
The political,
The hypocrites,
The spiritual –
The decided and
The ambivalent –
The benevolent,
The vindictive,
The achievers –
The over
And the under –
The eclectic,
The intolerant,
The open
And closed minded,
The narcissistic
And the altruistic,
Everyone breathing
Life in the moment.

I'm watching

Everyone

As they step up

To the window.

Then I realize

They're stopping

To glance

At the variety

Of animals

On the other side

Of the glass.

Crazy

Squash the tiny voices
Speaking nonsense –
No matter how loud
They scream,
The words are useless –

Like pinpricks,
Aggravation

Welcome to
A more sensible
Domination
Carrying us
Onward
And upward –
Though life
Doesn't transport us
In a straight line.

The underlying
Mischief
Doesn't tolerate
Sensible
Thought processes.

Tap into fear
With spontaneous
Hypothetic
Unrealistic
Situations.

There's a fine line
Between intelligent
And insane –
Someone holds
A ruthless mixture.

Beauty is
Poking the eye
Of the beholder.

Emerging

Taking a path
To face the consequences
(Is this the road
Less travelled?)

When thoughts become
Too comfortable
Silence steps in –
White noise squealing.

When does
The inner banter
Become self-fulfilling
Prophecy?
Today.

Dreaming With Open Eyes

Clock in
Eyes open
Getting ready
For another
Day alive.

Sun rises
Yet again –
Another one
Inhale, exhale
Stirring swiftly
The pot
Of grit,
Truly unavoidable.

The days
Join in,
Letting me
Know they
Are still
Here, unsettled.

Taking in
Another breath –
Stench received.

Cruise along
In commencing
The careful
Climb into
Morning's glory,
Chapter one
Today's story.

Flipping through
Various images
Of dreams –
Quickly deleting.

Not worrying
Beyond this
Intimate moment.

Standing outside,
Fresh air,
Not remembering
How or
Even when
I arrived
Out here.

Taking in
Another breath.

If this
Is what
Death's grip
Feels like,
Come and
Get me –
This is
Milder than
The horror
Stories promised.

Dogs barking
Bring me
Back here –
Dogs bark
Again, again…
Constantly setting
On nerves –

On the
Edge of
Falling apart.

Another breath
Of fresh
Air, unwavering
This time.

Test results

Not back –

Unready, unsteady

Not wanting

Mixed marks.

Battles rage

All over

The world,

This one

I claim

Before trying

To initiate

Once again.

Sleep deprived,

Feeling pain,

Glory in

The highest.

Please return

To sender

The bittersweet

Dreams clad

Unconscious awkwardness.

Another breath,

Deeply divisive.

Internal Peril

There may be pleasantries
In this world
Of damnation
But that's all
Sugar-coated
Sweet nothingness.

He fought in a war
A long time ago,
But sometimes feels
Like he just returned
Yesterday
With the post-traumatic
Anxiety attack.

Now he nurtures
The variety of beauty
In his floral garden –
Licking his internal wounds.

But there's misery,
A household
Of melancholy –
The results
Of battles
Continuing
To rage onward.

And nobody notices
Unless they're invited
To come a little
Closer, specifically
To come indoors.

Nobody really knows
Because the roses
And the geraniums
And the way
The pachysandra
Are laid out
Showing off
Splendor in hues
And aromas.

To bring the outside in
Without suppressing
That pain – rather
To find a release.
Might find cause
To open a door
Or, at least, a window –
Fresh air releases
The musty inner feeling

But there is something
About keeping
The critics pleased

By planting a
flower For them
In his garden.

Mental Well Being

Not everybody
Who sleeps here
Lives here.

Discerning
The difference
Between
Who is welcome
And who is not

Takes time.

Fade

There's a nightmare
That startled me
Awake
And already I can't
Remember the contents.

The sweat soaks
The edges
Of my hair
And my clothing.

I find the household
Unfazed and
Asleep still.
The dog remains
Motionless,
Slumbering
On the floor.

Why do I panic
Over nothing?
Why do I fear
The things inside
That truly
Create no harm?

Unless something
Deep within
Comes to
Fruition.

Maybe I am
Merely torturing
Myself
Subconsciously.

In the other room
I come to settle
For a little time
Away from everyone
Or everything.

Outside on the street,
A vehicle passes by
Carrying someone
With fears and joys,
Concerns and compliments,
Of their own.
They disappear
As quickly
As they arrive –
Unknowing of eyes
Watching from behind
Closed doors.

However, I held on to
Charming endearments
And grotesque treacheries
Of my own.
But what am I
Legitimately holding?
And for what purposes?

Before I find
A release,
I fall asleep
In this chair,
Clutching
To what I believe
Is mine
While holding out
For another day
When maybe
I could release
The demons.

And no unforgiving
Hallucinations
Will fill my mind
During daylight hours.
The darker vibe
Is removed

Temporarily –

For what it's worth.

Nirvana

Standing in the driveway –
    1 A.M.
        2 A.M.
Time doesn't matter –
But the sun is gone
And the moon is here
The only glow
Comes from lights
On the neighbor's
Front porches.

A vehicle would pass
Absent mindedly –
Roar of the engine,
Thump of the bass
Of the blaring music –
Never mind
That I see
What they don't.

One feline asleep
In various positions
Inside the house,
The canine asleep
On the floor
At the foot

Of the bed.

Another kitty boisterous
Somewhere else
Inside the house –
Maybe running
The length
Of the basement
In a sudden burst
Of enamored energy.

A breeze picks up
Carrying away
Whatever prayers
Are whispered
On the air
This night.

Appointed Time

This is better than
A lazy Sunday
Afternoon.
Before the early rise
Of an early mourning
And the world
Believing it comes
Alive, but in
A zombie-like
State of mind –
Blinded by the sun –
    Mortified without
        Knowing –
            Shocking!

But the darkness
Is not something
Of science fiction
Or of fantasy.
The world seems less
Polluted –
    The air
Is more pleasant
To inhale/exhale,
More space to move.

The predator is not
The moon.
    But
Instead, the sun.
The stars show victory.

This is not when
The high tribunal
Comes alive –
    This
Is when they sleep,
Still dreaming that
They are in command –
  The cancers
  Of society
  By the
  Daytime.

Now there is not
The time to answer
The social
complexities.

This is when
Heaven calls
In clarity
And the ability
To hear
Is plentiful.

Making eye contact

With the Beloved

Is smoother

Then the fumbling

Words of improvised

Supplications.

Reestablish

When the time comes
Who will bury
The last human?
Who will be present
To honor their souls
When all of humanity
Has reached the point
Of finality?

The places where
We once remembered –
The memorials
The historical
The monuments honoring
Human accomplishments –
Will some day
Be forgotten forevermore.

The places of persecution
And religious worship
And holy prayer
Will always remain in spirit
But nobody, no body will be there
To pay homage to that solitude.

The zany activities

The foolish antics –
No more.

The expectations –
Realistic or not –
The reputations –
Realistic or not –
Will no longer be.

What will bring us
To that point
Of conclusiveness?
That point being
The place where
We stop dying
But start living.

And we can begin
Once again
To memorialize
The breaths of lives.

Good Enough

We discussed God
While sweating
In the hot tub.

We claimed views
From experiences
From our fathers.

Others look on
Speculating within
On how this will end?

We throw in Hell –
Directing crooked fingers
– Are we there yet?

We each believe
What we say
To the other as truth.

We talk Heaven –
How we each will
Get there someday.

I say believe,
Have faith, truly
Through the redeemer.

He says, truthfully,
Being good, only,
Will get us there.

We become silent,
Indication of an impasse –
An awkward moment.

But giving us a moment
To hope neither of us
Are being good for nothing.

In A Room By The Window

Snow falls slightly,
Lightly – not quite misguided.

Looking inward,
A reconnection
With the past
Of better days –
Forgiving? Yes, that's shared.
Even as death lurks
Nearby, or looming overheard,
Or as a mythical monster
Lies in wait under the bed.

Maybe the window
Should stand open
For an easier escape.

Let the cold winds blow
But remain outside.

The bitter embers
Of pain are not stoked
These days –
Instead, replaced
With a light and warmth
More constant.

Until the better end

Waited long enough,
I've postponed change patiently
(at least in my mind's eye)
For the right moment
To emerge –
Not to bring splendor
To my name.
For my name
Is not worthy
Of admiration.
By the standards
Of this world,
I am not the beauty –
I am not the beloved –
But I, like you,
Am the benefactor.

This is the time
For me to emerge,
To speak up and to speak out,
Even if the sound comes out
As an exasperating squeal.
This is my joyful noise,
Out of tune,
And if that is the price

I pay, then let me pass.

Too much time has passed,
No matter how irrelevant –
No matter how irreverent.
The scars of the past
Are decorative, but are not
Here for defining purposes.

In my mind's eye,
I've waited patiently
Long enough.
But the timing
I see is not
The final remedy.

So Close

In the faint moonlight
A fly
Lies trapped
In death
On the windowsill.
Once screaming
For a getaway,
But could not
Be heard.
So very close –
    On the other side
    Of the window.
A screen –
    So very near
    To freedom.
The warm summer's
atmosphere Carries memories
Of having been there.
He died trying –
She died trying –
With dedication.

Doomsday

Why am I trying
To sleep with the dead
When I'm not yet tired?

Beauty

I poked the eye
Of the Beholder
Just to draw
Some attention.

That didn't work well.

I attempted punching
The eye
Of the Beholder.

That didn't work well either.

Instead, I stop pestering
The Beholder.
My attention
Is given
Elsewhere.

My children arrived,
Each receiving
A welcoming hug.

And I noticed
The Beholder
Gawking.

Defined

LOVE
      is a self-portrait
          of
GOD
    and we
        are the
IMAGE

'Til Death

The seven days of mourning
Have labored for seven years
And going on seven more.

When will the eighth day
Come? Bringing freedom!
Bringing resemblance of relief!

There is a lack of breathable air –
I am short of breath – rapid, fleeting –
Inside this coffin of time.

Just need to take breaths – slow, steady.
Concentrate. Concentrate. Concentrate.
It's so difficult to concentrate.

This must be a kind of trap.
There are loud banging noises
Like someone hammering nails.

The pounding is not uncommon.
But comes at irregular intermissions.
Sometime louder. Sometimes softer.

Someone is sending me early
To a grave, but aren't I

Already at that point?

The whispering in the pews
Becomes jumbled – grasping –
Carrying empty conversations.

Sanity

People
May say
I am crazy

No problem
Because
That may be
The only
Entity
Keeping me
Sane

When I'm Gone

I am merely
An interruption
Of this world.
An interruption
In this time –
Of the future
That once was
And of the past
That once will be.

Sometimes I wonder
Why I am here,
Or if anyone
Would understand
If I turned up missing
For a while.

But am I really
Here to care about
What other people
Think of me?
(Like if anyone,
Though, I hope
Nobody thinks poorly,
But I've realized
This is unavoidable.)

I want to take
A trip
Past the edge
Of town.

I've lost traction.
Then again,
Trying to climb
An icy slope
Will do that
Without
The proper tools.

This is my way
Of avoiding
Saying good-bye…
Just get up
And leave…
Slipping out
The back door
Without someone
Making a production…
Moving out
Of this mundane purgatory…
And sending myself
Adrift –

Which may be
More thrilling
In the random
Changing dynamics.

These feelings
May only be visceral,
That I may desire
Acting upon.

Lord have mercy.

Troubled Sleep

No matter how hard
I try to make things
Come together for the better,
The outcome shows I am
Cursed in making things worse.

I shouldn't let these demons
Encourage my mindset.
But these hands of mine
Are the ones carrying the load and
Caring for the final works of art.

The storm clouds dull the night sky
The rain's rhythms lock my fitful mind
Into an easy, deep slumber
Until thunder jostles me awake.
I stare, disturbed, into darkness.

Impressive

The day stands,
Waiting,
By the back door
Needing to be
Let out.

Looking at the door,
Then back at me,
Then at the door
Again.

There's a tiredness
But the desire
For an early morning
Adventure
Is essential.

Outside, a cat
Crosses the yard
Out of reach –
The dog finds
Excitable
Energy,
Unwarranted
From the depths.

The stray cat's

Done nothing –

Minding its own –

But stops

To figure out

The distracted canine,

Wondering if

There are connections

Before sliding away

Impeccably sincere,

In peace.

Come And Gone

We heard the sirens
Before the vehicles
Came up on us.
One vehicle, joyriding
Followed by the police —
Close, close….so close
But not close enough.

My neighbor and I
Heard the warnings
While working
Underneath
My vehicle.
The transmission
Was falling apart.

We saw them
Make the turn,
Coming up
Our street –
All happening
In slow motion –
A scene seen
On television
Or in the movies.

We stop to watch,
Unsure
Of what to do.
A 2-door coupe
Followed by two
State troopers.

They blew through
The stop sign
At the corner,
Making a wide turn.

As quickly as
They interrupted
Our quiet lives,
They were gone.

We looked at each other,
Shrugged our shoulders,
And got back
Under the vehicle –
The transmission fluid
Finally drained out.

The sirens have died,
The chaos has ended,
At least for now.

We are left

Not knowing

The outcome –

Such is life

Sometimes.

Reliability

He's wanted
To stand out,
To be
An individual –
To be
One of a kind –
To be.

But even
Individuals
Need a sense
Of purpose,
A desire
To fit in.

The stars
Accurately aligned,
Shining with vigor
No matter how
Dull or void
Or null. Oh boy!
Each one
A part
Of something
Greater
Then themselves.

The magnitude
Can't necessarily
Be seen
By the naked eye.

He walks the night
Without destinations
Or distractions
Or distinctions
In sight
Or in mind.

Steps are not
In meticulousness.
Waking from one side
Of the sidewalk
To the other,
From one side
Of the street
To the other.
Not taking corners
In an exact
Turns of 90 degrees.
Nothing is precise –
Except God
And God's creations.

Just as long

As he gets

Somewhere

In the end –

Relying on

God, the stars,

The moon,

A few

People along

The way,

And,

In a few hours,

The sun.

Almost

Long ago
The optimism
I once held dear
Became barren
And lay spread eagle
For all to see,
Flayed open
For all to disparage.

Now seen
In the later
Stages
Of decomposition
Having been
Sprawled out
At great length –

The spirit within,
Once so vast
So deep
So wide,
Has shriveled
Smaller than
With each
Passing day.

"Almost" is
Never enough –
Getting close
Is not quite
Sufficient.

Sitting under the moon
That is not quite full
Doesn't hold
The same effect.

There's constantly
Something missing –
Just a sliver,
Just a little,
Just not justifiable.

Being good enough
Doesn't make
A person great,
But nobody says,
"Thank you
For being
Average."

Should

Trying to make the most of it –
The most of what? –
This life that's been dealt.
Somewhere along the way
The choices I made were affecting
The outcome of where I am today.

And the "What if…" questions
Begin to nag at me again,
Leaving to wonder what could've
And should've and might've been.

The headstones of some moments
Are worn and tilted – forgotten.
Others have yet to be placed
On the freshly packed earth.

But dwelling on those voices
Only eat away at the time
That I could be, should be,
And might as well be doing
Something entirely different
Then that which I am now.

Like Thoughts Crowding My Mind

The cat starts
By weaving
Around my feet.
I ignore her,
Trying to silence
My thinking.

Thriving for
Attention,
The cat jumps upon
The table
In front of me,
Voicing her
Opinions
As if she
Dances
With the
Overthinking.

She twists and turns
Before rolling over
Onto her back
To let me know
It is alright
To rub her belly –

An act of trust.

And soon enough
She's had her share
Of play time.
She jumps off
The table
And scurries away.

Planting herself
On the windowsill
On the other side
Of the room
In curious
Inclination.

Purring contentment.

And eventually
The cat will
Come back,
Interrupting
The silence
Of what is given
Of the night.

Inevitable

I watch the time
Listlessly and persistently
Moving in stride
From now to whenever.

Each second passing
Is like raindrops,
Except in perfect
syncopation In life's
overflowing puddle.

Each breath digs
The shallow grave
A little bit more
Superficially.

Life

God's not dead –
Maybe I'm not
In the proper
Place to hear
Any breathing.

Or just maybe
I have no
Way of knowing
How to get
A pulse.

Wayne City

The town sleeps,
Closed early
Last evening
And won't open again
Until Monday.

The people here
Take the day
Of rest seriously.

All vehicles out
Usually parked
At the local
Churches of God
Or brunch places.

The house that lived
On the edge of town –
Where the family used to watch
Vehicles
Leave town
As quickly as
They arrived –
Now sits as
An empty lot.

From the front porch

That used to be,

They'd sit

Watching – knowing

Who was who.

But sometimes

They didn't recognize

The out of towners –

Family visiting family,

Or unwelcome

Characters

Needed rushing

Out of town.

However,

Tonight,

The world

Within

The city limits

Sleeps.

Unknowingly

Which residents

Will arise.

Mystical Fish

When reality sets in
And I finally realize
I am unable to swim
In this life(less) pool,
I may attempt
Floating for a time.
My tired muscles
Needing a rest.

I will spend the time
On my back, looking
Towards the lonely heavens
That are looking back at me –
Do the heavens understand
What they are watching?
Probably better than most.

Is paradise frowning
On the life I've endured? Is it
Because I have not started
Fully filling the calling
On this lifeline of mine
Is supposed to accomplish?
Is this life truly mine?
Maybe there is sadness
By the fact I'm stopping.

Stopping? Or waiting?
Or appearing to give up?

There is an absence
I sense – greater than
The void between
The clouds. My mind
Veers off, trying to fill
The space where a sinking
Feeling overwhelms me,
Drowning my soul.

Is it finished?

Three Oh Five

Sorry for my tardiness –
I experienced the unfortunate
Event of stepping barefoot
On smoldering embers.

Eventually I limped
To my favorite chair,
My beloved spot
Near the window

Where I am able
To see the world –
You may be
Correct to believe
There are
No affective life
Experiences
From this position,
But this place
Becomes my little
World this morning.

This time
Tomorrow
May be very
Different.

But I'm not
There –
Not yet –
And I'm not
Fretting until then.

Worrying steals sleep –
From daydreams and
Nightmares alike.

Bitter

I don't like artificial flavors
And this smile is a façade.

My spirit is in a debt
That is overflowing
From deep within, like
A fountain turning
Into a waterfall turning
Into a swelling river turning
Into muddy floodwaters.

There is sabotage in my life –
Admittance is the first step,
Isn't it? I am tired of living
Unconsciously, having gone numb
And on the brink of spiritual death.

I'm tired of suppressing passions
And of the growing discomforts
As a result. Then hunger pangs
Commence – unnoticed in the beginning,
Followed by explosions of bitterness.

Tired of living in someone else's
Glossed over fabrications
That appear like certainty.

I need tangible truth. I need these deceits
To fall by the wayside and burn away.

Collected

Trying to remain calm
But the excitement
Of chasing the tail
Without means to an end
Is befitting
Until I understand, later,
What is happening.

The complexity
Of the situation is not fully
comprehended In the dizzying midst
Of the running around
In circles.

While repressing the emotion
As to not awaken
The neighborhood
Takes equivocal respect.

And a sigh of relief
Long before the sun rises.

Room Without A View

The emptiness is overwhelming
But God comes to fill this void
But is God not strong enough
To enter from outside these walls.
Or am I too stubborn
To tear them down to allow
God's appearance?

There is no knock on the door.
Then again, there is no door.
There is no point crying out
Since there is no way out (or in).
I'd take pride in workmanship
With the exception that I now
Stand alone.

There is no conclusion to this.
Not yet anyways. I don't know
If there are search parties seeking
Or if anyone realizes they should seek
out. This room, then, becomes a coffin.
A slow suffocation for a painless end. No!
Not yet.

There is a voice whispering faintly,
Almost muted from the rush hour of panic

And unnecessary thoughts clogging the mind.
"I have my reasons" for breath, for life.
"Just wait for Me" – and I start cracking
Under the pressure of unfamiliar fortitude
Rising. Intensifying.

Paper Doll Princess

An apparition disturbs the peace –
A ghostly appearance, unknown
And exceptionally unnecessary.

This is not a welcome muse –
Merely lights dancing across
The walls from a passing vehicle?

Interrupting a darkened memory
The hands of time are beat
Through and through with arthritis.

One dog remained on the floor
While the other sleeps on the bed,
Not fazed by quiet moments slipping.

Death pinches at the heels
Of the tornado
Destroying inner peace.

There is no release without some pain –
Tearing away pieces here and there –
Repressing memories through mindful amputations.

Wiping away sleep from my eyes,
A subconscious performance
That slips quickly into the night.

Limited by unlimited compromises
This cannot be the best coping mechanism –
An effort in remembering, wanting to forget.

This has not become a euphoric ecstasy
In the night after night of mindful visits –
Or is this mindless? Or, rather, heartless?

There is nothing gracious in this moment.
Just an invasion of privacy – detestable!
Officially destroying the nocturnal silence.

This image – haphazard on the wall –
Fades for another night, a mystery
And a misery that will appear again.

There is hope that this fabricated vision
Will stay away longer…much longer.
Between visits – always unwelcomed.

Someone may blame these moments
On a sinful, demonizing history, but
This could happen to anyone, at any time.

A sassy embezzlement of a corrupt mind!
Forget corrupt – this is human thought processes.
No matter how (in)secure throughout.

This is when the relapses happen – in times
Of idle hands – in times for breaking free, remaining busy –
In times of frailness, breaking images louder than ever.

A derivative of the schizophrenic mind –
A major setback attempting to play a minor role –
Who controls the stage, the settings, and players?

Laughter happens as notions siphoned
From inside the head into spoken bitterness
Or written phrases flung onto unread pages.

The delusions considered happy thoughts
In some parts of the world (the lowest points) –
Moving out, swaying into a lullaby, and back to sleep.

Delicious and delicate ways to snooze,
Slowly recoiling, so as not to jump into the depths –
The last of rush hour traffic at day's end.

A welcoming home, of sorts – exploited.

Rest

Coaxing order out of turmoil
As an inter-dimensional escape
From the current reality

During a sleepless night,
Graffiti on the soul appears
Chaotic to the untrained eye

There is something sacred, or
Curious, or both, in a series
Of moments cascading peacefully

The rain stops. The clouds dissipate.
All appears well with the world
Based in this time/space continuum.

Cleansing

The storm lords itself
Over everyone equally.
The rains are unleashed
At an appointed time,
Catching some by surprise –
  Feet hitting the ground
  As people run for cover.
Not all are fond of moments
Such as these, but others
Find reassurance in such times.
The waters drenching –
This is the crowning glory,
With the exception
Of the lightning and thunder,
All the dirt swims away,
A natural springtime baptism.
Someone who wasn't ready
Shakes a clenched fist
And curses the skies (heavens).
The thunderclaps, then rolls endlessly,
As if in response. There is joy
Coming in the conclusion, not the concussion.
The ending comes when the gray skies
Decrescendo into a distant memory
Someone holds on to for dear life.

No Doubt

God believes
In me
More than
I do
In Him.

S.O.S.

I wish I could
Do this
On my own,
But I can't –
An affable smile
Isn't worth
The energy.

So, I whisper
God's name
Into the dark

And while
Waiting
For the morning
Rush hour
God
      whispers
           back.

138

We've trekked together
For many miles.
We've seen injustices
And various atrocities.

We're providing them
With food, drink –
Burning fires to
Lift their spirits.

Our feet hurt
From much walking
Along the road
Considered less traveled.

We must rest –
Rejuvenate our souls
For the adventures
Of coming days.

I sit, landing
Like a rock
Fallen from great
Heights – grunting – sigh

You, my friend,
Quickly join me,
Still energized mightily –
Fresh consuming fire.

"I don't expect
Anything more today,"
I say, humbly
(So I thought).

"You've done great
And wonderful things.
I need nothing
More than that."

The smile grows
Upon your face
And I sense
A gentle reprimand.

Calmly, you speak –
Apart from me
You can do
Nothing. Understand? Nothing.

Though not everyone
Is clean enough.
The betrayal lays

Murky under foot,

Unwashed and stained
Thick with sludge.
I have confidence
In you, brother.

The reconcilable rock
Will profoundly meet
The most levelheaded
By humbling yourself.

Sitting in juxtaposition
Of your precedent,
I thoroughly understand
The underlying command.

That we cannot
And should not,
Do life alone
But intimately equal

Jeremy

Sitting outside
On the tailgate
Of my pickup truck,
Summer night breezes
Kick up softly
Every now and then.
But we hardly notice.

He shares with me
His story, his past.
The portion of his existence
Continues to haunt him,
Sometimes keeping
Him up late at night –
Even after many years.

He questions if time
Really heals all wounds,
Or if the scars trigger
Digging up buried
Dilapidation.

He could have turned out
Differently than he has.

Maybe he should have

Turned out differently
Based on various statistics –
Based on skin color.
Based on age.
Based on family dynamics,
Socio-economic status,
Group memberships,
Political affiliations (or afflictions),
Elitism (or lack thereof),
Religious persuasion (or perversion)
Because data always shows
A greater chance of…

And he fulfilled a greater
Chance of that not occurring.

And in due time
He should have a moment –
    Of enlightenment,
    Of intervention
    Of freedom –
When God creates
A new world
For this young man.

Maybe next week
We will sit inside
The church instead

Of the church's parking lot
At 3 o'clock
In the morning.

Maybe next week
He will stand before
The church members
And proclaim
He's been released
Of the anger
And the frustration
And the terror
That's destroying him.

Maybe God will allow
Release of healing,
The walls broken down
Because of all the prayers
Provided for so long.

But this is about the people
Who have prayed.
It's about the young man
Sitting beside me
And his ability, eventually
To move on, to be released
And his opportunity
To stand like Peter

As a rock,
A cornerstone
For others
Who also scuffle
In the mental dynamics
Of good versus evil.

For tonight, though,
He has more time
To not cross over
That mountaintop.

Now is just
What he needs
To share his story.

Now is just.
Now is just.
Now is just…
Now is justified.

And I am
Attempting to wrap
My mind around
What has happened
To him.

For these precious moments,

The parking lot
Provides us the space
To understand where lines
Should have been drawn
Long ago.

Eventually, we'll be back
Inside.

Timely Touch

Standing at the window's ledge
Looking at the flowing street,
Clouded over across the sky –
Little hands pressed upon the pane
The little boy pats the rain.

Watching from nearby, this day,
Upon his son so dry,
The man stressed across no fear
As heaven passes through his soul –
Daddy sheds a tear.

Turning from his point of view
To find out who stands behind,
Father's little gentle man
Waves his comfort home
Through childhood Pat-a-pan.

Looking towards his child's charm,
Not wasting precious time
Driving through this shared day –
Angels embrace internally
As generations pat the sun.

Before The Dawn

God's blessing asks
"Have you written
About me today?"

The smile disappears
And sadness emerges
– "Not today," is
What I say.
"Not yet today."

Before I sleep
Tonight, I leave
In a preparation
For pleading mediation.
This very moment
Has become darkest…

Welcomes the light,
Cresting before long –
Giving an interruption
To the mourning.

Do not fret,
For there is
         Hope.

ACKNOWLEDGEMENTS

So many people have allowed me to succeed and fail throughout the process of the delivering of this book.

Special thanks to my parents, David and Laurel, for whom this book is dedicated. Also, a special thanks to Carrie and Allen, and their families. We've always taken the scenic route to get to every destination – and the journey to get here had its share of charming misdirections.

Special thanks to Stephen and Iko Blackmon, who were a guiding light in finding direction.

Honorary thanks to Ray and Helen – they loved us no matter what, supported us in our dreams, and were committed in being our biggest fans in the concerts of our lives. Honorary thanks to Leonard and Ruth – for showing us what it means to live and to laugh and to love. Very grateful the desire for poetry passed down through the genes. And the many thanks to family and friends through the adventures and inspirations.

Author BIO

Mark Maier is a poet with two new collections of poems, 13 8 and 3 A.M. Stories. These collected works are his first publications.

Mark grew up near Cleveland, Ohio. He graduated from Cleveland State University in 2000, where he was one of the student editors of their literary magazine.

After spending a couple years working in the newspaper industry in Ohio and Illinois, he found a niche working in the financial world as an accounting technician.

He holds a love for travel. He holds a fondness for attending poetry open mic nights – a mutual consideration of listening to poets impart their creations as well as revealing his works.

He currently lives in Columbus, Ohio with two cats.

Stay Connected With Mark

Go to https://dsmstoryforge.com/dsm-authors/mark-maier/ to get connected with Mark, follow him on social media, and see what else he is publishing and writing about these days!

www.ingramcontent.com/pod-product-compliance
Lightning Source LLC
Chambersburg PA
CBHW062117080426
42734CB00012B/2897